50 Breakfast Bliss Cooking for Home Recipes

By: Kelly Johnson

Table of Contents

- Classic Buttermilk Pancakes
- Blueberry and Lemon Muffins
- Cheesy Spinach and Egg Breakfast Casserole
- Banana Nut Bread
- Avocado Toast with Poached Eggs
- Sweet Potato Hash with Sausage
- Greek Yogurt Parfaits with Honey and Granola
- Cinnamon Swirl French Toast
- Breakfast Burritos with Chorizo and Veggies
- Apple Cinnamon Oatmeal
- Smoked Salmon Bagel with Cream Cheese
- Ham and Cheese Croissants
- Chocolate Chip Waffles
- Breakfast Tacos with Scrambled Eggs
- Berry Smoothie Bowl
- Eggs Benedict with Hollandaise Sauce
- Sweet Corn Fritters
- Maple-Glazed Bacon
- Shakshuka with Feta
- Pumpkin Spice Pancakes
- Vegan Tofu Scramble
- Quiche Lorraine
- Breakfast Pizza with Sausage and Cheese
- Chia Pudding with Fresh Fruits
- Spinach and Mushroom Omelette
- Breakfast Sandwich with Bacon and Avocado
- Cranberry Orange Scones
- Huevos Rancheros
- Sourdough Toast with Ricotta and Honey
- Maple Pecan Granola Bars
- Dutch Baby Pancake
- Breakfast Poutine with Gravy and Eggs
- Strawberry and Cream Crepes
- Savory Oatmeal with Fried Egg
- Protein-Packed Smoothie

- Hash Brown Casserole
- English Muffin Breakfast Sliders
- Zucchini Bread
- Sausage Gravy and Biscuits
- Coconut Rice Porridge
- Mediterranean Breakfast Platter
- Peanut Butter and Banana Toast
- Bagel Breakfast Sandwiches
- Fluffy Scrambled Eggs with Herbs
- Overnight Oats with Almond Butter
- Breakfast Salad with Soft-Boiled Egg
- Croque Madame
- Lemon Ricotta Pancakes
- Green Smoothie Breakfast Bowl
- Almond and Cranberry Breakfast Bars

Classic Buttermilk Pancakes

Ingredients

- 2 cups (250g) all-purpose flour
- 2 tablespoons granulated sugar
- 2 teaspoons baking powder
- 1 teaspoon baking soda
- 1/2 teaspoon salt
- 2 cups (480ml) buttermilk
- 2 large eggs
- 1/4 cup (60g) unsalted butter, melted and slightly cooled
- 1 teaspoon vanilla extract (optional)
- Butter or oil for cooking

Instructions

1. **Prepare the Dry Ingredients:**
   In a large mixing bowl, whisk together the flour, sugar, baking powder, baking soda, and salt.
2. **Mix the Wet Ingredients:**
   In a separate bowl, whisk the buttermilk, eggs, melted butter, and vanilla extract (if using).
3. **Combine the Wet and Dry Ingredients:**
   Pour the wet ingredients into the dry ingredients. Stir gently until just combined; a few lumps are fine. Overmixing can make the pancakes dense.
4. **Preheat the Pan or Griddle:**
   Heat a non-stick skillet or griddle over medium heat. Lightly grease with butter or oil.
5. **Cook the Pancakes:**
   Scoop about 1/4 cup of batter onto the pan for each pancake. Cook until bubbles form on the surface and the edges look set (about 2-3 minutes). Flip and cook the other side until golden brown (another 2 minutes).
6. **Serve Warm:**
   Stack the pancakes and serve with butter, syrup, fresh fruit, or your favorite toppings.

Blueberry and Lemon Muffins

Ingredients:

- 1 1/2 cups (190g) all-purpose flour
- 1/2 teaspoon baking powder
- 1/2 teaspoon baking soda
- 1/4 teaspoon salt
- 1/2 cup (100g) granulated sugar
- 1/4 cup (60g) unsalted butter, melted
- 1 large egg
- 1 teaspoon vanilla extract
- 1/2 cup (120ml) milk
- Zest of 1 lemon
- 1 1/2 cups (225g) fresh or frozen blueberries
- 1 tablespoon flour (for coating the blueberries)

Instructions:

1. **Preheat the Oven:**
   - Preheat your oven to 350°F (175°C). Line a muffin tin with paper liners or grease it lightly.
2. **Mix the Dry Ingredients:**
   - In a medium bowl, whisk together the flour, baking powder, baking soda, salt, and sugar.
3. **Prepare the Wet Ingredients:**
   - In a separate bowl, whisk together the melted butter, egg, vanilla extract, milk, and lemon zest.
4. **Combine the Wet and Dry Ingredients:**
   - Pour the wet ingredients into the dry ingredients and stir gently until just combined. Do not overmix.
5. **Add the Blueberries:**
   - Toss the blueberries in 1 tablespoon of flour to prevent them from sinking during baking. Fold them gently into the batter.
6. **Fill the Muffin Tin:**
   - Spoon the batter into the muffin tin, filling each cup about 3/4 full.
7. **Bake:**
   - Bake for 18-22 minutes, or until a toothpick inserted into the center of a muffin comes out clean.

8. **Cool and Serve:**
    - Allow the muffins to cool in the tin for 5 minutes, then transfer to a wire rack to cool completely. Enjoy!

Cheesy Spinach and Egg Breakfast Casserole

Ingredients:

- 1 tablespoon olive oil
- 1 small onion, diced
- 2 cloves garlic, minced
- 4 cups fresh spinach, chopped
- 1 1/2 cups shredded cheddar cheese
- 1 cup shredded mozzarella cheese
- 6 large eggs
- 1/2 cup milk
- 1/2 teaspoon salt
- 1/4 teaspoon black pepper
- 1/4 teaspoon paprika
- 1/4 teaspoon dried thyme

Instructions:

1. **Preheat the Oven:**
   - Preheat your oven to 375°F (190°C). Grease a 9x9-inch baking dish.
2. **Cook the Vegetables:**
   - Heat the olive oil in a large skillet over medium heat. Add the onion and garlic, and cook until softened, about 5 minutes. Add the spinach and cook until wilted, about 2-3 minutes. Remove from heat.
3. **Prepare the Egg Mixture:**
   - In a large bowl, whisk together the eggs, milk, salt, pepper, paprika, and thyme.
4. **Combine the Ingredients:**
   - Spread the spinach and onion mixture evenly in the prepared baking dish. Pour the egg mixture over the top, then sprinkle with shredded cheeses.
5. **Bake:**
   - Bake for 30-35 minutes, or until the eggs are set and the top is golden brown.
6. **Cool and Serve:**
   - Let the casserole cool for a few minutes before slicing. Serve warm and enjoy!

Banana Nut Bread

Ingredients:

- 1 1/2 cups (190g) all-purpose flour
- 1 teaspoon baking soda
- 1/4 teaspoon salt
- 1/2 cup (115g) unsalted butter, softened
- 1 cup (200g) granulated sugar
- 2 large eggs
- 4 ripe bananas, mashed
- 1/4 cup (60ml) milk
- 1 teaspoon vanilla extract
- 1/2 cup (60g) chopped walnuts or pecans (optional)

Instructions:

1. **Preheat the Oven:**
   - Preheat your oven to 350°F (175°C). Grease a 9x5-inch loaf pan.
2. **Mix the Dry Ingredients:**
   - In a medium bowl, whisk together the flour, baking soda, and salt.
3. **Cream the Butter and Sugar:**
   - In a large bowl, beat the butter and sugar together until light and fluffy.
4. **Add the Wet Ingredients:**
   - Add the eggs, one at a time, beating well after each addition. Stir in the mashed bananas, milk, and vanilla extract.
5. **Combine the Dry and Wet Ingredients:**
   - Gradually add the dry ingredients to the wet ingredients, mixing until just combined. Fold in the nuts if using.
6. **Bake:**
   - Pour the batter into the prepared loaf pan. Bake for 60-65 minutes, or until a toothpick inserted into the center comes out clean.
7. **Cool and Serve:**
   - Let the banana bread cool in the pan for 10 minutes, then transfer to a wire rack to cool completely. Slice and enjoy!

Avocado Toast with Poached Eggs

Ingredients:

- 2 ripe avocados, mashed
- 4 slices of whole-grain bread, toasted
- 4 large eggs
- 1 tablespoon white vinegar (for poaching)
- Salt and pepper to taste
- Red pepper flakes (optional)
- Fresh herbs (such as parsley or chives) for garnish

Instructions:

1. **Prepare the Poached Eggs:**
    - Bring a pot of water to a simmer and add vinegar. Crack each egg into a small bowl, then gently slide it into the water. Poach for about 3-4 minutes, until the whites are set but the yolks are runny. Remove with a slotted spoon and set aside.
2. **Prepare the Avocado Toast:**
    - Mash the ripe avocados with salt, pepper, and any desired seasonings.
3. **Assemble the Toast:**
    - Spread the mashed avocado on the toasted bread slices. Top each with a poached egg, sprinkle with red pepper flakes (optional), and garnish with fresh herbs.
4. **Serve:**
    - Serve immediately and enjoy!

Sweet Potato Hash with Sausage

Ingredients:

- 2 large sweet potatoes, peeled and diced
- 2 tablespoons olive oil
- 1/2 pound sausage, crumbled (your choice of type)
- 1 small onion, diced
- 1 red bell pepper, diced
- 1 teaspoon smoked paprika
- Salt and pepper to taste
- Fresh parsley, chopped for garnish

Instructions:

1. **Cook the Sweet Potatoes:**
    - Heat olive oil in a large skillet over medium heat. Add the diced sweet potatoes and cook until soft and lightly browned, about 10-12 minutes. Remove and set aside.
2. **Cook the Sausage:**
    - In the same skillet, cook the crumbled sausage over medium heat until browned, about 5-7 minutes. Remove any excess fat.
3. **Combine the Veggies and Sausage:**
    - Add the onion and bell pepper to the skillet with the sausage and cook until softened, about 5 minutes. Return the sweet potatoes to the skillet, add paprika, salt, and pepper, and toss to combine.
4. **Serve:**
    - Garnish with fresh parsley and serve hot!

Greek Yogurt Parfaits with Honey and Granola

Ingredients:

- 2 cups Greek yogurt
- 1 tablespoon honey
- 1/2 cup granola
- 1/2 cup fresh berries (blueberries, strawberries, or raspberries)

Instructions:

1. **Assemble the Parfaits:**
    - In individual cups, layer Greek yogurt, honey, granola, and fresh berries.
2. **Serve:**
    - Repeat the layers until the cup is filled. Serve immediately for a fresh, delicious breakfast!

Cinnamon Swirl French Toast

Ingredients:

- 4 slices cinnamon swirl bread
- 2 large eggs
- 1/2 cup milk
- 1/2 teaspoon ground cinnamon
- 1/4 teaspoon vanilla extract
- Butter for cooking
- Powdered sugar for dusting
- Maple syrup for serving

Instructions:

1. **Prepare the Egg Mixture:**
    - In a bowl, whisk together eggs, milk, cinnamon, and vanilla extract.
2. **Cook the French Toast:**
    - Heat a skillet over medium heat and add butter. Dip each slice of cinnamon swirl bread into the egg mixture, ensuring both sides are coated, then cook in the skillet until golden brown on both sides, about 3-4 minutes per side.
3. **Serve:**
    - Dust with powdered sugar and serve with maple syrup.

Breakfast Burritos with Chorizo and Veggies

Ingredients:

- 1/2 pound chorizo sausage, crumbled
- 1 bell pepper, diced
- 1 small onion, diced
- 4 large eggs
- 4 flour tortillas
- 1/2 cup shredded cheese (cheddar or Mexican blend)
- Salsa for serving

Instructions:

1. **Cook the Chorizo:**
    - In a skillet over medium heat, cook the chorizo until browned and fully cooked, about 7-8 minutes. Remove and set aside.
2. **Cook the Veggies:**
    - In the same skillet, cook the bell pepper and onion until softened, about 5 minutes. Add the eggs and scramble them until fully cooked.
3. **Assemble the Burritos:**
    - In each tortilla, layer the scrambled eggs, chorizo, cheese, and any other desired toppings. Roll up the tortillas into burritos.
4. **Serve:**
    - Serve with salsa on the side.

Apple Cinnamon Oatmeal

Ingredients:

- 1 cup rolled oats
- 2 cups milk or water
- 1 apple, peeled and diced
- 1 teaspoon ground cinnamon
- 1 tablespoon brown sugar (optional)
- Chopped nuts for topping (optional)

Instructions:

1. **Cook the Oats:**
    - In a pot, bring the milk or water to a boil. Add the oats, reduce the heat, and simmer for about 5-7 minutes, stirring occasionally.
2. **Add the Apples and Cinnamon:**
    - Add the diced apples and cinnamon to the oatmeal and cook for an additional 3-4 minutes, until the apples are tender.
3. **Serve:**
    - Stir in brown sugar if desired, top with nuts, and serve warm.

Smoked Salmon Bagel with Cream Cheese

Ingredients:

- 2 bagels, halved and toasted
- 4 ounces smoked salmon
- 1/4 cup cream cheese, softened
- 1 tablespoon capers (optional)
- 1/4 red onion, thinly sliced
- Fresh dill for garnish

Instructions:

1. **Prepare the Bagels:**
    - Toast the bagels and spread cream cheese on each half.
2. **Assemble the Bagel:**
    - Top with smoked salmon, red onion slices, capers, and fresh dill.
3. **Serve:**
    - Serve immediately for a delicious, savory breakfast.

Ham and Cheese Croissants

Ingredients:

- 4 croissants, split
- 4 slices ham
- 4 slices Swiss or cheddar cheese
- 1 tablespoon Dijon mustard (optional)

Instructions:

1. **Assemble the Croissants:**
    - Spread Dijon mustard (if using) on the inside of each croissant. Add a slice of ham and cheese to each croissant.
2. **Bake:**
    - Place the croissants on a baking sheet and bake at 375°F (190°C) for 10-12 minutes, or until the cheese is melted and the croissants are golden.
3. **Serve:**
    - Serve warm for a tasty breakfast treat.

Chocolate Chip Waffles

Ingredients:

- 2 cups all-purpose flour
- 2 tablespoons sugar
- 1 tablespoon baking powder
- 1/2 teaspoon salt
- 2 large eggs
- 1 3/4 cups milk
- 1/4 cup vegetable oil
- 1 teaspoon vanilla extract
- 1/2 cup chocolate chips

Instructions:

1. **Prepare the Waffle Batter:**
    - In a bowl, mix together flour, sugar, baking powder, and salt. In another bowl, whisk together eggs, milk, oil, and vanilla extract.
2. **Combine the Ingredients:**
    - Pour the wet ingredients into the dry ingredients and stir until just combined. Fold in the chocolate chips.
3. **Cook the Waffles:**
    - Preheat your waffle iron and lightly grease it. Pour the batter into the waffle iron and cook according to the manufacturer's instructions.
4. **Serve:**
    - Serve warm with maple syrup, whipped cream, or additional chocolate chips. Enjoy!

Breakfast Tacos with Scrambled Eggs

Ingredients:

- 4 small flour tortillas
- 4 large eggs
- 1/4 cup milk
- 1 tablespoon butter
- 1/2 cup shredded cheese (cheddar or Mexican blend)
- 1/4 cup salsa
- 1/4 cup avocado, sliced
- Fresh cilantro for garnish

Instructions:

1. **Scramble the Eggs:**
   - Whisk together eggs and milk. Heat butter in a skillet over medium heat, then pour in the egg mixture. Cook, stirring occasionally, until scrambled and just set.
2. **Assemble the Tacos:**
   - Warm the tortillas and fill each with scrambled eggs, cheese, salsa, avocado slices, and cilantro.
3. **Serve:**
   - Serve the breakfast tacos immediately for a fresh and flavorful meal.

Berry Smoothie Bowl

Ingredients:

- 1 cup mixed berries (strawberries, blueberries, raspberries)
- 1/2 banana
- 1/2 cup Greek yogurt
- 1/4 cup almond milk
- 1 tablespoon honey or maple syrup
- Toppings: granola, chia seeds, coconut flakes, fresh berries

Instructions:

1. **Blend the Smoothie:**
    - In a blender, combine berries, banana, Greek yogurt, almond milk, and honey. Blend until smooth and creamy.
2. **Serve:**
    - Pour the smoothie into a bowl and top with granola, chia seeds, coconut flakes, and fresh berries.

Eggs Benedict with Hollandaise Sauce

Ingredients:

- 4 English muffin halves, toasted
- 4 large eggs
- 4 slices Canadian bacon
- 1 tablespoon vinegar (for poaching eggs)
- 1/2 cup unsalted butter, melted
- 3 large egg yolks
- 1 tablespoon lemon juice
- Salt and pepper to taste

Instructions:

1. **Poach the Eggs:**
    - Bring a pot of water to a simmer and add vinegar. Crack the eggs into individual bowls, then gently slide into the water. Poach for 3-4 minutes, then remove with a slotted spoon.
2. **Make the Hollandaise Sauce:**
    - In a heatproof bowl, whisk together egg yolks and lemon juice. Gradually whisk in the melted butter until thick and smooth. Season with salt and pepper.
3. **Assemble the Benedict:**
    - Place a slice of Canadian bacon on each English muffin half, top with a poached egg, and drizzle with hollandaise sauce.
4. **Serve:**
    - Serve immediately for a classic, indulgent breakfast.

Sweet Corn Fritters

Ingredients:

- 1 cup corn kernels (fresh, frozen, or canned)
- 1/2 cup all-purpose flour
- 1 teaspoon baking powder
- 1/2 teaspoon salt
- 1/4 teaspoon ground black pepper
- 1/4 cup milk
- 1 large egg
- 2 tablespoons chopped cilantro
- Vegetable oil for frying

Instructions:

1. **Prepare the Fritter Batter:**
    - In a bowl, combine corn, flour, baking powder, salt, pepper, milk, egg, and cilantro. Mix until well combined.
2. **Fry the Fritters:**
    - Heat vegetable oil in a skillet over medium heat. Drop spoonfuls of the batter into the hot oil and fry for about 2-3 minutes on each side, until golden brown.
3. **Serve:**
    - Drain on paper towels and serve warm with sour cream or salsa.

Maple-Glazed Bacon

Ingredients:

- 12 slices bacon
- 1/4 cup pure maple syrup
- 1 tablespoon Dijon mustard
- 1/2 teaspoon ground black pepper

Instructions:

1. **Cook the Bacon:**
   - Preheat the oven to 400°F (200°C). Place the bacon slices on a baking sheet lined with parchment paper and bake for 12-15 minutes, or until crispy.
2. **Prepare the Glaze:**
   - In a small bowl, whisk together maple syrup, mustard, and pepper.
3. **Glaze the Bacon:**
   - Brush the cooked bacon with the maple glaze and return to the oven for an additional 2-3 minutes to caramelize.
4. **Serve:**
   - Serve the maple-glazed bacon warm as a sweet and savory side dish.

Shakshuka with Feta

Ingredients:

- 2 tablespoons olive oil
- 1 onion, diced
- 1 red bell pepper, diced
- 2 cloves garlic, minced
- 1 can (14 oz) diced tomatoes
- 1 teaspoon ground cumin
- 1/2 teaspoon paprika
- Salt and pepper to taste
- 4 large eggs
- 1/4 cup crumbled feta cheese
- Fresh parsley for garnish

Instructions:

1. **Prepare the Sauce:**
    - Heat olive oil in a skillet over medium heat. Sauté the onion, bell pepper, and garlic until soft. Add the diced tomatoes, cumin, paprika, salt, and pepper. Simmer for 10 minutes until the sauce thickens.
2. **Cook the Eggs:**
    - Make wells in the sauce and crack the eggs into the wells. Cover and cook for 6-8 minutes, or until the eggs are cooked to your liking.
3. **Serve:**
    - Top with crumbled feta and garnish with fresh parsley. Serve with crusty bread for dipping.

Pumpkin Spice Pancakes

Ingredients:

- 1 1/2 cups all-purpose flour
- 1 tablespoon brown sugar
- 1 teaspoon baking powder
- 1/2 teaspoon baking soda
- 1/2 teaspoon salt
- 1 teaspoon ground cinnamon
- 1/2 teaspoon ground nutmeg
- 1/4 teaspoon ground ginger
- 1 cup canned pumpkin puree
- 1 cup buttermilk
- 1 large egg
- 1 tablespoon melted butter

Instructions:

1. **Prepare the Pancake Batter:**
   - In a bowl, whisk together flour, sugar, baking powder, baking soda, salt, and spices. In a separate bowl, combine pumpkin, buttermilk, egg, and melted butter. Pour the wet ingredients into the dry and stir until just combined.
2. **Cook the Pancakes:**
   - Heat a skillet or griddle over medium heat. Lightly grease with butter or oil. Pour 1/4 cup of batter onto the skillet and cook until bubbles form, then flip and cook until golden brown on the other side.
3. **Serve:**
   - Serve with maple syrup, whipped cream, and a sprinkle of cinnamon.

Vegan Tofu Scramble

Ingredients:

- 1 block firm tofu, drained and crumbled
- 1 tablespoon olive oil
- 1/4 teaspoon turmeric
- 1/4 teaspoon smoked paprika
- Salt and pepper to taste
- 1/4 cup nutritional yeast (optional)
- 1/2 cup chopped spinach or kale
- 1/4 cup diced tomatoes

Instructions:

1. **Prepare the Tofu:**
    - Heat olive oil in a skillet over medium heat. Add the crumbled tofu, turmeric, paprika, salt, and pepper. Cook for 5-7 minutes, stirring occasionally.
2. **Add Veggies:**
    - Stir in the spinach or kale and tomatoes. Cook until the greens are wilted and the tofu is heated through.
3. **Serve:**
    - Sprinkle with nutritional yeast, if using, and serve with toast or as a filling for wraps.

Quiche Lorraine

Ingredients:

- 1 pre-baked pie crust
- 1/2 pound bacon, chopped
- 1/2 cup onion, diced
- 1 cup shredded Gruyère or Swiss cheese
- 4 large eggs
- 1 cup heavy cream
- Salt and pepper to taste
- Fresh parsley for garnish

Instructions:

1. **Cook the Bacon:**
    - In a skillet, cook the bacon over medium heat until crispy. Remove and set aside. Drain excess fat.
2. **Prepare the Quiche Filling:**
    - In the same skillet, sauté the onion until softened. In a bowl, whisk together eggs, heavy cream, salt, and pepper. Stir in the cheese, bacon, and onions.
3. **Assemble the Quiche:**
    - Pour the filling into the pre-baked pie crust and bake at 375°F (190°C) for 30-35 minutes, or until the quiche is set.
4. **Serve:**
    - Let the quiche cool slightly before slicing. Garnish with fresh parsley and serve warm.

Breakfast Pizza with Sausage and Cheese

Ingredients:

- 1 pizza dough (store-bought or homemade)
- 1/2 cup pizza sauce
- 1 cup cooked breakfast sausage, crumbled
- 1 cup shredded mozzarella cheese
- 1/2 cup shredded cheddar cheese
- 2 large eggs
- Fresh herbs for garnish (optional)

Instructions:

1. **Preheat the Oven:**
   - Preheat the oven to 475°F (245°C). Roll out the pizza dough onto a baking sheet or pizza stone.
2. **Assemble the Pizza:**
   - Spread pizza sauce over the dough. Sprinkle cooked sausage and both cheeses evenly on top.
3. **Add Eggs:**
   - Create small wells in the cheese and crack an egg into each well.
4. **Bake the Pizza:**
   - Bake for 10-12 minutes, or until the crust is golden and the eggs are set to your liking.
5. **Serve:**
   - Garnish with fresh herbs and serve immediately.

Chia Pudding with Fresh Fruits

Ingredients:

- 1/4 cup chia seeds
- 1 cup almond milk (or any milk of choice)
- 1 tablespoon maple syrup
- 1/2 teaspoon vanilla extract
- Fresh fruit (berries, mango, banana) for topping

Instructions:

1. **Prepare the Chia Pudding:**
   - In a bowl, mix chia seeds, almond milk, maple syrup, and vanilla extract. Stir well and let sit for 5 minutes.
2. **Refrigerate:**
   - Cover the bowl and refrigerate for at least 2 hours or overnight to thicken.
3. **Serve:**
   - Top with fresh fruit and serve chilled.

Spinach and Mushroom Omelette

Ingredients:

- 2 large eggs
- 1/4 cup spinach, chopped
- 1/4 cup mushrooms, sliced
- 1 tablespoon butter
- Salt and pepper to taste
- Shredded cheese (optional)

Instructions:

1. **Sauté the Veggies:**
    - In a skillet, melt butter over medium heat. Sauté mushrooms until soft, then add spinach and cook until wilted.
2. **Prepare the Omelette:**
    - Whisk eggs with salt and pepper. Pour over the veggies in the skillet and cook until the eggs set. Optionally, add cheese before folding.
3. **Serve:**
    - Fold the omelette in half and serve warm.

Breakfast Sandwich with Bacon and Avocado

Ingredients:

- 2 slices whole wheat or white bread, toasted
- 2 slices cooked bacon
- 1/2 avocado, mashed
- 1 fried egg
- Salt and pepper to taste

Instructions:

1. **Assemble the Sandwich:**
    - Spread mashed avocado on one slice of toast. Add bacon, fried egg, and the other slice of toast.
2. **Serve:**
    - Season with salt and pepper and serve immediately.

Cranberry Orange Scones

Ingredients:

- 2 cups all-purpose flour
- 1/2 cup sugar
- 2 teaspoons baking powder
- 1/2 teaspoon baking soda
- 1/2 teaspoon salt
- 1/2 cup unsalted butter, cold and cubed
- 1 cup dried cranberries
- Zest of 1 orange
- 1/2 cup heavy cream

Instructions:

1. **Preheat the Oven:**
    - Preheat the oven to 400°F (200°C). Line a baking sheet with parchment paper.
2. **Make the Dough:**
    - In a bowl, whisk together the dry ingredients. Cut in the cold butter until the mixture resembles coarse crumbs. Stir in cranberries and orange zest.
3. **Shape and Bake:**
    - Add the cream and stir until just combined. Form into a dough, flatten it, and cut into wedges. Bake for 18-20 minutes or until golden.
4. **Serve:**
    - Let cool slightly before serving.

Huevos Rancheros

Ingredients:

- 2 corn tortillas
- 2 large eggs
- 1/2 cup salsa
- 1/4 cup refried beans
- 1/4 cup shredded cheese (cheddar or Mexican blend)
- Fresh cilantro for garnish

Instructions:

1. **Cook the Eggs:**
   - In a skillet, cook eggs sunny side up or to your liking.
2. **Prepare the Tortillas:**
   - Warm the tortillas in another skillet or microwave.
3. **Assemble the Dish:**
   - Spread refried beans on each tortilla, top with salsa, a cooked egg, cheese, and cilantro.
4. **Serve:**
   - Serve warm with extra salsa on the side.

Sourdough Toast with Ricotta and Honey

Ingredients:

- 2 slices sourdough bread, toasted
- 1/2 cup ricotta cheese
- 2 tablespoons honey
- Fresh fruit (optional)

Instructions:

1. **Toast the Bread:**
    - Toast the sourdough bread until golden brown.
2. **Assemble:**
    - Spread ricotta cheese on each slice of toast, drizzle with honey, and top with fresh fruit if desired.
3. **Serve:**
    - Serve immediately for a quick, sweet breakfast.

Maple Pecan Granola Bars

Ingredients:

- 2 cups rolled oats
- 1/2 cup chopped pecans
- 1/4 cup maple syrup
- 1/4 cup peanut butter
- 1/4 teaspoon vanilla extract
- 1/4 teaspoon salt

Instructions:

1. **Prepare the Mixture:**
    - In a bowl, mix oats, chopped pecans, maple syrup, peanut butter, vanilla extract, and salt until well combined.
2. **Press and Chill:**
    - Press the mixture into a lined baking pan and refrigerate for 1 hour.
3. **Cut and Serve:**
    - Cut into bars and store in an airtight container.

Dutch Baby Pancake

Ingredients:

- 3 large eggs
- 1/2 cup all-purpose flour
- 1/2 cup milk
- 1 tablespoon sugar
- 1/4 teaspoon salt
- 2 tablespoons unsalted butter
- Powdered sugar for dusting
- Fresh fruit or syrup for topping

Instructions:

1. **Prepare the Batter:**
   - In a bowl, whisk eggs, flour, milk, sugar, and salt until smooth.
2. **Cook the Pancake:**
   - Preheat the oven to 425°F (220°C). Heat butter in a cast-iron skillet over medium heat. Pour in the batter and bake for 20-25 minutes until puffed and golden.
3. **Serve:**
   - Dust with powdered sugar and top with fresh fruit or syrup. Serve immediately.

Breakfast Poutine with Gravy and Eggs

Ingredients:

- 2 cups frozen French fries, cooked
- 2 large eggs
- 1/2 cup sausage gravy
- 1/4 cup shredded cheddar cheese
- Fresh parsley for garnish

Instructions:

1. **Prepare the Fries:**
    - Cook the French fries according to package directions, or fry them to golden perfection.
2. **Cook the Eggs:**
    - Fry the eggs to your desired doneness (over-easy or sunny-side-up work well).
3. **Assemble the Poutine:**
    - Place the cooked fries on a plate, pour over the warm sausage gravy, and top with the fried eggs. Sprinkle with shredded cheese and garnish with parsley.
4. **Serve:**
    - Serve immediately for a hearty and indulgent breakfast.

Strawberry and Cream Crepes

Ingredients:

- 1 cup all-purpose flour
- 1 tablespoon sugar
- 1/2 teaspoon vanilla extract
- 1 cup milk
- 2 large eggs
- 1 tablespoon melted butter
- 1/2 cup heavy cream
- 1 tablespoon powdered sugar
- 1 cup fresh strawberries, sliced

Instructions:

1. **Make the Crepes:**
    - Whisk together flour, sugar, vanilla, milk, eggs, and melted butter. Heat a non-stick pan over medium heat and pour in a small amount of batter, swirling to form a thin layer. Cook for 1-2 minutes, then flip and cook another 30 seconds. Repeat with remaining batter.
2. **Prepare the Cream:**
    - Whip the heavy cream and powdered sugar until stiff peaks form.
3. **Assemble the Crepes:**
    - Place a crepe on a plate, top with whipped cream and sliced strawberries, then roll it up.
4. **Serve:**
    - Serve immediately for a sweet and light breakfast treat.

Savory Oatmeal with Fried Egg

Ingredients:

- 1/2 cup rolled oats
- 1 cup vegetable broth
- 1 tablespoon butter
- 1/4 cup shredded cheese
- 1 fried egg
- Salt and pepper to taste
- Fresh herbs for garnish

Instructions:

1. **Cook the Oatmeal:**
    - Bring vegetable broth to a simmer and stir in the oats. Cook until tender, about 5 minutes. Stir in butter and cheese, then season with salt and pepper.
2. **Cook the Egg:**
    - Fry an egg in a skillet to your desired doneness.
3. **Assemble the Dish:**
    - Spoon the oatmeal into a bowl, top with the fried egg, and garnish with fresh herbs.
4. **Serve:**
    - Serve hot for a savory, filling breakfast.

Protein-Packed Smoothie

Ingredients:

- 1 banana
- 1/2 cup Greek yogurt
- 1 tablespoon almond butter
- 1 scoop protein powder
- 1/2 cup almond milk
- 1 tablespoon chia seeds
- Ice cubes (optional)

Instructions:

1. **Blend the Ingredients:**
   - Place banana, Greek yogurt, almond butter, protein powder, almond milk, and chia seeds into a blender. Add ice cubes for a thicker texture.
2. **Blend Until Smooth:**
   - Blend until smooth and creamy.
3. **Serve:**
   - Pour into a glass and serve immediately for a refreshing, protein-packed breakfast.

Hash Brown Casserole

Ingredients:

- 1 bag frozen hash browns
- 1/2 cup sour cream
- 1 can cream of mushroom soup
- 2 cups shredded cheddar cheese
- 1/2 cup chopped green onions
- Salt and pepper to taste

Instructions:

1. **Prepare the Mixture:**
    - In a large bowl, combine hash browns, sour cream, cream of mushroom soup, shredded cheese, and green onions. Season with salt and pepper.
2. **Bake the Casserole:**
    - Transfer the mixture to a greased baking dish and bake at 350°F (175°C) for 45-50 minutes, until golden and bubbly.
3. **Serve:**
    - Let cool slightly before serving.

English Muffin Breakfast Sliders

Ingredients:

- 4 English muffin halves
- 4 large eggs
- 4 slices cheddar cheese
- 4 sausage patties, cooked
- Butter for toasting
- Salt and pepper to taste

Instructions:

1. **Toast the Muffins:**
    - Butter and toast the English muffin halves in a skillet until golden brown.
2. **Cook the Eggs:**
    - Fry the eggs in a skillet, seasoning with salt and pepper.
3. **Assemble the Sliders:**
    - Place a slice of cheese on the bottom half of each muffin. Add a sausage patty, fried egg, and top with the other muffin half.
4. **Serve:**
    - Serve warm for a hearty breakfast slider.

Zucchini Bread

Ingredients:

- 2 cups all-purpose flour
- 1 teaspoon baking powder
- 1/2 teaspoon baking soda
- 1/2 teaspoon salt
- 1 teaspoon cinnamon
- 2 large eggs
- 1 cup sugar
- 1/2 cup vegetable oil
- 2 cups grated zucchini
- 1 teaspoon vanilla extract
- 1/2 cup chopped walnuts (optional)

Instructions:

1. **Preheat the Oven:**
    - Preheat the oven to 350°F (175°C) and grease a loaf pan.
2. **Prepare the Wet Ingredients:**
    - In a bowl, whisk together eggs, sugar, oil, zucchini, and vanilla extract.
3. **Combine Dry Ingredients:**
    - In another bowl, combine flour, baking powder, baking soda, salt, and cinnamon. Gradually fold the dry ingredients into the wet ingredients.
4. **Bake the Bread:**
    - Pour the batter into the prepared pan and bake for 55-60 minutes, or until a toothpick comes out clean.
5. **Serve:**
    - Let cool before slicing and serving.

Sausage Gravy and Biscuits

Ingredients:

- 1 package biscuit dough (or homemade biscuits)
- 1 pound breakfast sausage
- 2 tablespoons all-purpose flour
- 2 cups milk
- Salt and pepper to taste

Instructions:

1. **Cook the Sausage:**
    - Cook the sausage in a skillet over medium heat until browned. Remove excess grease.
2. **Make the Gravy:**
    - Add flour to the sausage, stirring to form a roux. Gradually add milk, whisking until thickened. Season with salt and pepper.
3. **Bake the Biscuits:**
    - While the gravy is cooking, bake the biscuits according to package directions or until golden brown.
4. **Serve:**
    - Pour the gravy over the biscuits and serve warm.

Coconut Rice Porridge

Ingredients:

- 1 cup jasmine rice
- 2 cups coconut milk
- 1 tablespoon honey
- 1/2 teaspoon vanilla extract
- Fresh mango slices (optional)

Instructions:

1. **Cook the Rice:**
    - In a pot, combine rice, coconut milk, and honey. Bring to a simmer and cook for 15-20 minutes, stirring occasionally, until rice is tender and the porridge has thickened.
2. **Finish the Porridge:**
    - Stir in vanilla extract and adjust sweetness with more honey if desired.
3. **Serve:**
    - Serve warm, topped with fresh mango slices or other fruit if desired.

Mediterranean Breakfast Platter

Ingredients:

- 1/2 cup hummus
- 1/2 cup tzatziki sauce
- 1/4 cup kalamata olives
- 1/4 cup cherry tomatoes, halved
- 1 cucumber, sliced
- 2 hard-boiled eggs, halved
- Pita bread, cut into wedges
- Feta cheese, crumbled

Instructions:

1. **Prepare the Ingredients:**
    - Arrange hummus, tzatziki, olives, tomatoes, cucumber slices, and hard-boiled eggs on a platter.
2. **Add the Pita:**
    - Warm the pita bread and cut it into wedges.
3. **Garnish:**
    - Sprinkle crumbled feta cheese over the platter.
4. **Serve:**
    - Serve the Mediterranean platter as a refreshing and wholesome breakfast.

Peanut Butter and Banana Toast

Ingredients:

- 2 slices whole-grain bread, toasted
- 2 tablespoons peanut butter
- 1 banana, sliced
- Honey (optional)
- Cinnamon (optional)

Instructions:

1. **Toast the Bread:**
   - Toast the slices of bread until golden brown.
2. **Spread the Peanut Butter:**
   - Spread peanut butter evenly on each toast.
3. **Add the Banana:**
   - Top with banana slices.
4. **Garnish:**
   - Drizzle with honey or sprinkle cinnamon for extra flavor.
5. **Serve:**
   - Serve immediately as a quick and nutritious breakfast.

Bagel Breakfast Sandwiches

Ingredients:

- 2 bagels, split
- 2 eggs
- 2 slices cheese (cheddar or American)
- 2 cooked sausage patties or 2 strips of bacon
- 1/4 avocado, sliced
- Salt and pepper to taste

Instructions:

1. **Prepare the Bagels:**
   - Toast the bagels until golden brown.
2. **Cook the Eggs:**
   - Fry the eggs to your desired doneness, seasoning with salt and pepper.
3. **Assemble the Sandwiches:**
   - Place a slice of cheese on the bottom half of each bagel. Add the cooked sausage or bacon, followed by the fried egg and avocado slices. Top with the other bagel half.
4. **Serve:**
   - Serve immediately as a filling breakfast sandwich.

Fluffy Scrambled Eggs with Herbs

Ingredients:

- 4 large eggs
- 2 tablespoons milk or cream
- 1 tablespoon butter
- Fresh herbs (parsley, chives, or dill)
- Salt and pepper to taste

Instructions:

1. **Prepare the Eggs:**
   - In a bowl, whisk together eggs, milk or cream, and a pinch of salt and pepper.
2. **Cook the Eggs:**
   - Melt butter in a non-stick pan over medium heat. Pour in the egg mixture and gently stir with a spatula until the eggs begin to set, then continue stirring to achieve fluffy scrambled eggs.
3. **Add Fresh Herbs:**
   - Once cooked, sprinkle fresh herbs over the eggs and adjust seasoning as needed.
4. **Serve:**
   - Serve immediately for a soft and fluffy breakfast.

Overnight Oats with Almond Butter

Ingredients:

- 1/2 cup rolled oats
- 1/2 cup almond milk
- 1 tablespoon chia seeds
- 1 tablespoon almond butter
- 1 teaspoon maple syrup (optional)
- Sliced almonds or fresh fruit for topping

Instructions:

1. **Prepare the Oats:**
    - In a jar or container, combine oats, almond milk, chia seeds, and maple syrup. Stir well to combine.
2. **Refrigerate Overnight:**
    - Cover the container and refrigerate overnight to allow the oats to soften.
3. **Add Toppings:**
    - In the morning, stir in almond butter and top with sliced almonds or fresh fruit.
4. **Serve:**
    - Serve chilled as a creamy and nutritious breakfast.

Breakfast Salad with Soft-Boiled Egg

Ingredients:

- 2 cups mixed greens (spinach, arugula, or baby kale)
- 1 soft-boiled egg, peeled and halved
- 1/2 avocado, sliced
- 1/4 cup cherry tomatoes, halved
- 1 tablespoon olive oil
- 1 teaspoon balsamic vinegar
- Salt and pepper to taste

Instructions:

1. **Prepare the Salad:**
   - Toss the mixed greens, cherry tomatoes, and avocado slices in a bowl.
2. **Add the Egg:**
   - Place the soft-boiled egg halves on top of the salad.
3. **Dress the Salad:**
   - Drizzle with olive oil and balsamic vinegar, then season with salt and pepper.
4. **Serve:**
   - Serve immediately as a fresh and nutritious breakfast.

Croque Madame

Ingredients:

- 2 slices of French bread
- 2 tablespoons Dijon mustard
- 2 slices ham
- 2 slices Swiss cheese
- 1 egg
- 1 tablespoon butter
- 1/4 cup grated Gruyère cheese

Instructions:

1. **Prepare the Sandwich:**
    - Spread Dijon mustard on one side of each slice of bread. Layer one slice with ham and Swiss cheese, then top with the second slice of bread.
2. **Cook the Sandwich:**
    - Heat a skillet over medium heat and melt butter. Grill the sandwich on both sides until golden brown and the cheese is melted.
3. **Fry the Egg:**
    - In the same skillet, fry an egg to your desired doneness.
4. **Assemble the Croque Madame:**
    - Place the fried egg on top of the sandwich and sprinkle with grated Gruyère.
5. **Serve:**
    - Serve immediately for a classic French breakfast.

Lemon Ricotta Pancakes

Ingredients:

- 1 cup ricotta cheese
- 1 cup all-purpose flour
- 1 teaspoon baking powder
- 1/4 teaspoon salt
- 1 tablespoon sugar
- 2 large eggs
- 1/2 cup milk
- Zest of 1 lemon
- 1 tablespoon lemon juice
- Butter for cooking

Instructions:

1. **Prepare the Pancake Batter:**
   - In a bowl, whisk together ricotta, eggs, milk, lemon zest, and lemon juice. In a separate bowl, mix flour, baking powder, salt, and sugar.
2. **Combine Wet and Dry Ingredients:**
   - Gradually add the dry ingredients to the wet mixture, stirring until just combined.
3. **Cook the Pancakes:**
   - Heat a skillet over medium heat and melt a small amount of butter. Scoop about 1/4 cup of batter per pancake and cook for 2-3 minutes on each side until golden.
4. **Serve:**
   - Serve warm with syrup, fresh berries, or powdered sugar.

Green Smoothie Breakfast Bowl

Ingredients:

- 1 frozen banana
- 1/2 cup spinach
- 1/2 cup almond milk
- 1/4 cup Greek yogurt
- 1 tablespoon chia seeds
- 1 tablespoon peanut butter
- Toppings: granola, fresh berries, coconut flakes, or nuts

Instructions:

1. **Blend the Smoothie:**
    - In a blender, combine frozen banana, spinach, almond milk, Greek yogurt, chia seeds, and peanut butter. Blend until smooth.
2. **Assemble the Bowl:**
    - Pour the smoothie into a bowl and top with granola, fresh berries, coconut flakes, or nuts.
3. **Serve:**
    - Serve immediately for a refreshing and healthy breakfast.

Almond and Cranberry Breakfast Bars

Ingredients:

- 1 cup rolled oats
- 1/2 cup almond butter
- 1/4 cup honey
- 1/4 cup dried cranberries, chopped
- 1/4 cup sliced almonds
- 1/4 teaspoon vanilla extract
- Pinch of salt

Instructions:

1. **Prepare the Mixture:**
    - In a bowl, combine oats, almond butter, honey, dried cranberries, sliced almonds, vanilla extract, and a pinch of salt. Stir until well mixed.
2. **Press into a Pan:**
    - Line an 8x8-inch baking pan with parchment paper. Press the mixture into the pan, spreading it evenly.
3. **Chill:**
    - Refrigerate for at least 2 hours to allow the bars to set.
4. **Cut into Bars:**
    - Once set, cut into squares or bars and serve as a quick breakfast snack.
5. **Serve:**
    - Serve chilled or at room temperature.